Anonymous

Souvenir Song Book

25 original Songs and Poems

Anonymous

Souvenir Song Book
25 original Songs and Poems

ISBN/EAN: 9783337176402

Printed in Europe, USA, Canada, Australia, Japan

Cover: Foto ©ninafisch / pixelio.de

More available books at **www.hansebooks.com**

PREFACE

In presenting to our Boys in Blue this pamphlet of original songs
and poems, the compiler begs to state that he has endeavored to
obtain the best and most diversified collection possible. It has
been his aim to have represented in this book the various re-
giments of the Eighth Army Corps.

For the benefit of our readers we give here an explanation of the
significance of the emblems on the Filipino flag and coat-of-
arms which are on the cover. The red, white, and blue of the
flag are respectively emblematic of the blood spilt in the cause
of Liberty, the purity of Liberty, and the blue sky which covers
all Liberty. The three stars represent the three rebellious islands of Luzon, Viscayas and Mindanao. The eight rays of the
central emblem represent the eight provinces of these islands
Finally, the mountain on the coat-of-arms represents Biac-na-ba-to,
or "Stone-cut-in-two, the place where the afterwards violated
treaty was signed between the Spaniards and the Filipinos.

The artistic and typographical work in this pamphlet has been
done by Filipinos.

That this pamphlet may prove an acceptable souvenir of the days
spent in Manila by our American soldiers, is the earnest wish of
the compiler.

J. D. Mitchell.

Manila, P. I. Nov. 1 st 1898.   Publisher.

Note. These songs and poems are published by permission of
the authors.

DEWEY, KING OF THE SEA.

Air—"Prodigal Son."

Oh I we have a bold sailor in Manila Bay ·
    We have, we have.
He captured the whole place in half a day
    He did, he did.
The gunners they made every shot tell
While they were not troubled by a single shell.
Remember the Maine and give them hell
    Sang Dewey the king of the sea   (repeat)

They avenged our boys who were killed on the Maine
    They did, they did
The Spaniards wont try dirty tricks again
    They wont, They wont
When Dewey sailed in to Manila Bay
A short time a go on the first of May
The Spaniards found it was moving day
    Sang Dewey the King of the sea   (repeat;)

Our gallant ships slipped through their lines
    They did, They did
They sailed right over the harbor mines
The gunners were primed with American rum
They dodged and juggled each bursting bomb
Sent three hundred Spaniards to Kingdom come
    Sang Dewey the King of the Sea   (repeat)

The batteries started to fire their shells
    They did, They did,
But into the water each one fell
    It did, It did,
Then the Flag-ship turned her ugly snout
And her forward turrets commence to shout
We'll give em some points on how to shoot
Sang Dewey the King of the Sea   (repeat)

A Torpedo boat came out with a dash
    It-did, It-did,
It started for Dew·y like a flash
    It-did, It-did,
Not a man at his post was seen to flinch
The Commander gave the button a pinch.
Let go his 12 pounders—Oh; what a cinch
    Sang Dew·y the King of the Seas,   (repeat)

All this took place on the first of May
    It did, It did,
Troops in ships w·re hurried away
    They were, They w·re,
Re-enforced by batteries H and K
John Astor's battery started away
And they hurried them on to Manila bay
    Sang Dewey the King of the sea   (repeat)

H·rd it was for me to wait
    It was It was.
I am glad they did not come too late,
    I am, I am.
The Newport is anchored here in the bay
So w·'ll start the ball when ever you say,
    Sang Dewey the King of the sea   (repeat)

H·w anxious I was a bout your boat
    I was, I was,
She was the richest prize a float
    She was She was
To Spanish soil and tropic seas
They hurried you on by every means
With the Governor of the Philipines
    Sang Dewey the King of the sea   (repeat)

Now the four expeditions came in safe and sound
    They did, They did,
Entren·hments the Spaniards w·re planting around
    They w·re, They were,
Since the 13th of August they re planting no more

They've learned what they never knew before
Entrenchments can't stop The 8th Army Corps
    Sang Dewey the King of the sea,   (repeat)

The eighth Army Corps I'll never forget
        I won't, I won't,
They put up a fight that was hot you bet,
        It was, It was,
We've driven our foes from land and sea
We all have shared in the victory
In this glorious fight for humanity
    Sang Dewey the King of the sea   (repeat)

Charles C. Webster

Astor Battery, U. S. A.

THE VOLUNTEER.

Let poets sing the many joys all caused by Capid's Dart.
Let those who may declare the praise of Science and of Art,
Of all the many pleasures great which fill this earthly Sphere,
It is the acme of my bliss to be a Volunteer:

„To arm ! to arms !" the country cries, and quick he heeds the call !
T o rally round the Stars and Stripes he hies him great and small,
Toplant the flag on foreign shores, and travel o'er the sea,
While others stay behind and yell:" Just give them hell for me.

He's off, and o'er the briny deep the stately vessel spins,
Gone are alas his noble dreams, and now the fun begins,
So grave and serious he finds the charge he has to keep,
That all else that his system holds he empties in the deep.

For many weary days and nights he travels o'er the brine:
By day he's cooped up on the deck scorched by the bright sunshine,
By night, within his little bunk he's forced to lie and smother.
Still patiently he grits his teeth and thinks of home and mother

T''is now he finds how sweet it is to live a soldier's life:
He's w. kened up at early dawn by the bugle, drum and fife;
He nimbly runs up stairs on deck expecting to remain,
But scarce a moment passes ere he's ordered down again !

He finds that military life, alas, is far from sweet.
His only joy is when he dreams he gets enough to eat
And if a storm should strike, the ship, or some slight wind should
swerve her,
He madly rushes round the deck and grabs a life preserver !

On land the story is the the same, no rest his soul can gain
He celebrates the wee small hours by fighting in the rain,
By day, wrapped up in flannel suits he sits around and sweats,
And makes out requisitions for light clothes he never gets !

So lives our noble Volunteer ! and when the war is o'er
And once again he sets his feet on old Columbia's shore,
He finds he's habit's creature, he has lost all sense and tact,
And shocks his friends by showing that he don't know how to act.

If to assuage his thirst he now should wander to the bar
He practices a little trick he's brought back from afar:
He drinks his beer, then at the man he slowly winks his eye;
The while he seeks the door and says "Denero" bye and bye !

And gone are his domestic tastes: his bed he seeks no more,
He breaks his poor old mother's heart by sleeping on the floor
He calls his sister moocher: his manners are the worst,
And when he hears the dinner bell he yells; "what squad eats first?

Oh all may sing the glory great of being a Volunteer!
But when again the Country calls, we'll all be deaf I fear
We "Il climb up on the street car roof the suckers for to see
An I as they pass we too will yell; "Just give them hell for me !

O. H. Fernback.
1st California U. S.

BATTLE SONG OF UTAH.

Air—"Marching—through Georgia."

Clear the guns for action boys, we are brave and strong and true,
Rouse and do the noble deeds you came so far to do.
Strike a blow of vengeance for our murdered boys in blue,
While we are fighting at Manila.

Chorus—Hurrah! hurrah! for Utah and her crew,
Hurrah! hurrah! for Pennsylvania too.
We'll give them what we said we would, when first we donned the blue!
While we are fighting at Manila.

Take your lanyards in your hands, the Spaniards are in sight,
Like our gallant Commanders we're spoiling for a fight,
For our cause is mighty and we know that we are right,
While we are fighting at Manila.

Take your aim with steady nerves, their colors soon must fall.
Utah boys you cannot rest till Old Glory's on the wall
With Pennsylvania at your side, have no fear at all,
While we are fighting at Manila.

While the shells were falling fast, our rounds were numbered, too
A bugle sounded in the rear with us the regulars, too,
'T was then that Freedom's cry arose to welcome comrades true,
While we were fighting in Manila.

Soon the Yankees won the day, the Spaniards th y drove back
Failure was their just reward for that midnight attack,
Utah's sturdy boys in blue, will ne'er be driven back
While there's fighting in Manila.

Chorus—Hurrah! hurrah! for Utah and her crew,
Hurrah! hurrah! for Admiral Dewey too,
We'll soon enjoy the glories boys, we all have won so true,
While we're returning to Utah.

Frank T. Hines
Utah Battery U. S. V.

THE OLD ARMY HARD-TACK.

How dear to my heart are the war-time mementoes
I've cherished in memory of sorrows and joys,
In the days when I tramped through the streets of Manila,
And splashed through the mud with the rest of the boys.
I've a rusty old knife I never will part with,
An old compaign hat and a jacket of blue,
A battered canteen, and a haversack holding
Some squares of the hard-tack we all had to chew
    Chorus— The Iron-bound hard-tack,
           The mould-covered hard tack
   The old army hard tack we all had to chew.

There was hard-tack from wars of the past generation
Which remained un consumed till this late Spanish war
T'is rumored that some which defied mastication,
Were marked "Civil war" or the stamp "B. C." bore !
What a triumph this is for the skill of the baker,
Indestructible product, defyng times tooth
But it conld not resist the assaults of our grinders,
The grinders we had in the days of our youth.
    Chorus There was 1812 hard-tack
         And '62 hard-tack
   The old army hard-tack we ate in our youth

Oh! youth can make feasts of the coursest of viands,
And never again shall we veterans feel
Such a zest in our lives, as we felt in this late war
When hard tack sufficed to create a square meal,
And tho'we may dine at more sumptuous tables,
We'd gladly exchange all the dainties they yield
For the hearty enjoyment and youthful digestion
That seasoned the hard-tack we ate in the field
    Chorus—The bullet'proof hard-tack
         The petrified hard-tack
   The old army hard-tack we ate in the field.

              Fred. Blake.
              Utah Battery, U. S. V.

BEHIND THE TRENCHES

Dedicated to the 1st California Volunteers, commemorating
July 31 st 1898.
(Air—"On the banks of the Wabash.")

From behind the trenches comes the gleam of rifles,
In the distance they can see the Spanish lines,
All around the tropic night is calm and peaceful,
While between the clouds above the full moon shines,
The palm leaves rustle feebly in the sea breeze,
And transient gleams the firefly here and there:
Calm and cool our gallant boys are waiting,
To avenge the Wrongs of home and country fair.

Chorus

Oh the honor of our grand old Stars and Stripes, boys,
Ne'er was tarnished since the hist'ry of its birth,
And will go unstained in ages yet to come, boys,
As long as there are men of loyal worth.

While these sturdy lads were peering o'er their breastworks,
As they strained their eyes to search the brush beyond,
To their mem'ry comes the scenes of early childhood,
And the picture of a loving mother fond;
And stouter yet grew every sturdy soldier,
Each grasped his rifle firmer in his hand,
As he thought of her who to his heart was dearest—
He was there fight for her and native land.

But are long this calm and peaceful scene of nature
Is transformed to one of noisy storm and strife;
At once the night of strained and anxious watching,
Has become an awful hell with carnage rife;
Above their heads the Spanish shells are screaming
While all around there spits a hail of lead,
Death's messengers are reaping in their harvest,
And here and there are stacked the sheaves of dead.

And while this fierce and bloody fight was raging,
All the elements in harmony warred too, .
Above the cannon could be heard the thunder roaring,
While the howing wind a fearful typhoon blew.
But they listed not, Columbia's martial heroes,
For in each breast there spent a fiercer storm—
The thougt of all the insults paid Old Glory,
The memory of which was ever warm.

They w re thirk'ng of the heroes foully slaughtered
Of injustice heaped upon their country brave,
Where their loved ones calm and patiently were waiting
Thus they made resolve for triumph or the grave.
When morning came pariah dogs were skulking,
The heavens once again were clear and blue,
Another day upon the war had broken,
On another vict'ry for our boys in blue.

CHORUS

On the honor of our grand old Stars and Stripes, boys,
Ne'er was tarnished since the hist'ry of its birth,
And't wul go unstained in ages yet to come, boys,
As long as there are men of loyal worth.

Frank Geere.
1st Wyoming U. S. V.

IN MANILA, 1998.

Through the streets of old Manila
    Aimlessly one day I strode
Till I bumped against a figure
    Standing silent in the road:
Such an odd ungainly figure
    That I quickly staggered back
Thinking that it was a spirit
    And I'd run across is's track.

On his head he wore a helmet
    Rather doubtful as to hue;

On his legs some battered leggins
  And his coat was once a blue.
On his shoulder was a musket
  Rusted with the rust of years
Like himself; this apparition
  Greatly served to rouse my fears.

"What the dickens are you?" asked I
  And my breath came quick and short.
He then out of force of habit
  Brought his rifle to the port
"You remember then," he answered,
  Just a hundred years ago
There was trouble with the Spaniards,
  'Twas about the Maine, you know.

Then I left home for Manila
  With more U. S. Volunteers
We were numbered several thousand
  All enlisted for two years
Oh! the others? they are sleeping
  In the ancient church yard here
Far from home and loving kindred
  And their native country dear

Some were stricken by diseases
  Victims of the fever's rage
Some were smitten by the small-pox
  Others died of ripe old age
I'm the last of all those thousands
  Through this place I still must roam
Waiting for expected orders,
  Welcome orders to go home!

                    W. O'Connell McGeehan.
                    Ist California U. S. V.

COLORADO'S ADVANCE ON MANILA.
August 13 th 1898.

When the bugle call was sounded
   We were ready every man,
Do you think that any faltered?
   Not a one but took his stand.
We'd been waiting there in silence
   When we heard the joyful note—
A yell went up to heaven.
   From every Soldier's throat.

And with springy step we bounded
   O'er our breast works to the fray.
Not a man was there who lingered,
   Not a man who cared to stay.
And with exultation beaming
   From each noble soldier's face
Each one vieing with his comrade——
   . To be first one in the race.

Forward! On ! Through mud and water
   We were eager for the fray.
We were bound to reach the trenches
   ' Where the hostile Spaniards lay.
Though we heard the bullets whistling
   Though we heard the cannons roar
Onward! Swifter! Was our motto .
   For Old Glory was before.

But the harder that we pressed them
   Faster still the Spaniards fled.
Leaving all of their equipments—
   Leaving all their wounded, dead.
When we saw Old Glory waving
   O'er Malate's stony wall,
We then vowed before the night came
   That Manila too must fall.

Forward! March ! The word was given
  And with a determined tread
We were bound to be victorious
  Or be numbered with the dead.
But the boastful Spaniards wilted
  Ere the fight was well begun.
O'er the walls of old Manila
  Soon a flag of truce was run.

Oh ! Spain where are your fabled heroes
  Are your days of conquering o'er?
You are now despised by nations
  That you ruled so long before.
Now I'll write for you a watch word,
  And its meaning I'll make plain,
"Uncle Sam" you must remember
  And dont forget the *Maine*.

                    Geo; F. Taylor.
                    1st Colorado U. S. V.

BATTLE OF MALATE.

It was July, the thirty-first,
The day dawned bright and clear
When orders rang throughout the Camp,
To buckle on our gear;
For Colonel Hawkins "Fighting Tenth"
Out to the front must go,
In all that band there was not one
Who feared the Spanish foe.

  To the front, we bravely marched,
With battle cry and song,
For in each manly soldier's breast,
Revenge for Spanish wrong;
Yes; of the "Maine," that fiendish crime,
Where hundreds of our braves
By Spaniards hellish treachery,
Were sent beneath the waves.

Now at the front, we are at last,
From Camp three miles away.
Neath pouring rain and scorching sun,
We labored through the day;
While the spiteful Mauser cracked,
And whistling balls came near,
Still bravely did we boys work on,
We never thought of fear.

Yes, bravely did we work that day,
While down the rain did pour,
We, with shovels, piled the sand
Three hundred yards or more;
In evening at the set of sun,
Many a boy did say,
"I am so tired, how well I'll sleep,
By old Manila Bay"

As night came on, we boys lay down,
Each seeking sweet repose,
Thinking not of a battle near,
Nor of the Spanish foes;
We loved to dream of home so dear,
Across the mighty Main,
In future time we hoped to be,
With loved ones there again.

Peacefully did each one sleep on,
Wrapped in dream's sweet charms,
Until there came a startling cry,
It was the call "To Arms!"
We flew to arms, our little band,
Nor did it take us long,
On front and flank the Spaniards were,
Full thirty hundred strong.

They opened with a murderous fire,
While fast the raindrops fell.
Into our ranks sent whistling balls,
Many a screaming shell,

But, what cared we, the "Fighting Tenth,"
We feared no death, no pain,
For in our ears still rang the cry,
"Boys, don't forget the Maine."

And firmly did we stand our ground,
Into the foe we poured,
A leaden hail, both thick and fast,
While Utah's cannon roared;
Three times they charged upon our lines,
Three times we drove them back,
While many cheers rang loud and clear,
Above the rifle's crack

"Fight on My Boys"| Pap Hawkins cried,
"As your fathers did before,
For we could never stand defeat,
Upon a foreign shore,"
We opened on the foe again,
And soon our work was done,
Spanish guns had ceased their fire,
And we the victory won.

Night passed at last a dismal night,
Yet, more dismal was the morning,
For with it came a drenching rain,
On dead and wounded pouring;
Many a soldier sat about,
His head upon his breast,
Grown weary from the work of night
Had sought a moments rest.

In that hour of our gloom,
We heard a bugle blast.
Many a heart leaped for joy,
Relief had come at last;
As other troops had come to take
Our cheerless place so damp,
While we in broken lines and files,
Went slowly back to camp.

—— 14 ——

Yes, slow'y did we wind our way,
As many hearts were sore,
For six of our brave boys were dead,
Wounded were many more;
Back to the Camp we bore our dead
Our fallen comrades dear,
While down each manly soldier's cheek,
Flowed many a silent tear.

That afternoon in Martial Shroud.
We laid our dead to sleep,
In conquered soil, by gentle hands,
Where Angels "Vigil' keep;
In a foreign land, they'd fought to free.
From slavery's yoke and chain,
A noble, yet downtrodden race,
From cruel, cruel Spain.

"Sleep on, Brave Boys Sleep on,"
Your work you've nobly done,
No nation forth to battle sent,
A truer, braver son;
In after years, when strangers stand,
Beside your hallowed grave,
They'll think of you, of how you died,
Your country's flag to save.

But, brighter still, there waits for thee,
Reward beyond the skies,
It is far brighter and more grand,
Than any earthly prize;
A happy place, where all will meet,
And never more to roam,
The heart once sad, will there be glad,
For we'll meet the loved at home.

In after years, when we shall meet,
On each "Memorial Day,"
Let's not forget our comrades dead,
Near "Old Manila Bay";

But drop a flower from every hand,
A fragrant blossom sweet,
In mem'ry of the boys who fell
In the "Battle of Malate."

J. A. Harshman.
10 th Pennsylvania U. S. V.

THE BOYS OF H" AND "K.

Oh we're the fighting bateiries; we are, we are,
And we're as brave as brave can be, we are, we are,
We came from far across the main
To lower the pride of haughty Spain,
That we were in for it was plain:
The boys of ' H" and "K '— the boys of ' H" and "K"

The boys in the trenches calmly slept, they did, they did,
While up the Spaniards softly crept, they did, they did,
They did not expect the foe about,
And their ammunition soon gave out
When the greasers were timely put to rout
By the boys of ' H" and "K' —the boys of 'H ' and ' K"

Oh! we got the call on Sunday night, we did, we did,
And grabbed our guns all ready for fight, we did, we did,
We piled right up through the rain and sleet,
And hurried on the foe to meet
They let no grass grow under their feet,
These boys of ' H" and "K"— the boys of ' H" and "K"

The shot and shell came thick and fast, they did, they did,
And we ducked our heads as they flew past, we did, we did
As they hit the trees with a nasty thud,
And splashed around us in the mud
We could see the enemy wanted the blood
Of the boys of ' H" and "K"— the boys of 'H" and "K"

But we were brave as crazy Turks, we were, we were,
And safely got behind the works, we did, we did,

You could hear our rifles go blankety blank,
As we let them have it from over the bank,
And kept the greasers from making a flank
On the boys of "H" and "K"—the boys of "H" and "K"

And so our batteries won the fight, they did, they did,
They put the enemy all to flight, they did
And they saved the bacon of many a lad
Who little a chance would ever have had
With happy hearts they cheered like mad
The boys of "H" and "K"—the boys of "H" and "K"

Edw. Ellis Pollock.

3 rd Artillery, U. S. A.

A LONELY SOLDIER.

"Only sittin' by th' railin,
Gazin' in th' glassy swell,
Fer th' moon is up an' sailin'
Under skies thet's like a bell
No, I aint got nothin' ailin',
Jest a kind o' dreamin' spell.

"Seems to me, when I'm a thinkin',
Thet th' waves slip out o' sight,
An' th' stars go off a winkin'
Into little dots o' light;
An' I see my Willie drinkin'
From his mug o' milk at night.

"Then, when foamy water swishes
From the troop--ship's risin' bows,
'Tseems like Mary's shiny dishes,
Er a line o' Sunday clothes,
White! I guess so! how I wishes,
I could see how collars goes.

"Fer I'm gittin' sort o' grimmy
On this jammed-up transport-ship

Mary'd hev some soap to gi' me,
Say! I' d take a jolly dip !
Then she'd bring the shears an' trim me
O' these whiskers on my lip.

"Fer she used to ketch an' hold me,
When they got to grcwin' rough,
Kind o' laughin' like, an' scold me
Cause I looked so' tarnel tough,
Then, her arms about, she'd fold me,
Till she'd clipped 'em smooth enough.

"Tehy's a thousand kinds o' action
I have seen th, dear gal try,
Down to given' me her fraction
O' her juicy pumpkin' pie
Durn my soul plum to distraction,
They's a winker in my eye !

"An' I kncw thet she's a prajin',
Fore the earliest light is come,
Till the lambs is out an' playin'
When the shadders fall an' gloam,
An' them lazy cows is strayin'
From the creek, an wanderin' home.

„All these things come rushin' to me,
As I'm lookin' in the brme,
An' the thought comes creepin' through me,
Thet she's in the water—shine;
Thet her soul is there to woo me
Up to things thet is divine."

Ira Kellogg.
Ist Nebraska U. S. V.

NEBRASKA'S BATTLE SONG
Air—"Dixie"

Oh, the plainsmen's sons to the war have gone
They've put their belts and blouses on
And they'll not retreat till the cause is won
    But fight and die for glory.
And the bards shall sing in the time to come
How the marshalled soldiers marched from home
To dig for wrong a gory tomb
    And this shall be their story

(REFRAIN)

All hail our gallant warriors.
    Hurrah, hurrah!
For freedoms land they boldly stand
And live or die in glory
    Hurrah, hurrah.
All hail our loyal army"

In the dead of night, on a foreign strand,
A thousand leagues from their native land,
    The soldiers hear war's wild command
      Adown the wood land ringing
Then they rise in rank on the battle field
With their arms laid bare and muscles steeled
And from hearts like oak that cannot yield
    A noble song is springing,

(REFRAIN)

"All hail our noble country.
    Hurrah, hurrah!
For freedoms land her sons will stand,
    And live or die in glory.
    Hurrah, hurra!
All hail our royal banner.

In the soldiers home-land far away
Are loving hearts that yearn and pray
For the warrior's safe return some day
    From scenes of strife and battle;
Then they'll lift the unstained banner high,
And shout as the strife--worn troops pass by;
And loud and long will sound the cry,
Above the war--drums rattle

(REFRAIN)

"All hail our flag and army
        Hurrah, hurrah!
For freedoms land, we'll join the hand
    And shout a loud hosanna
        Hurrah, hurrah!
All hail our deathless banner."

                    Ira Kellogg
                    1st Nebraska U. S. V.

THREE CHEERS FOR ALL

Three cheers for the boys who were near the bay,
Who waited patiently by the way,
To help if needed to win the day,
While fighting before Manila.

Three cheers for the boys who were at the front,
Who bore the heat of the battles brunt,
And heard Deaths messengers musical hunt
While fighting before Manila.

Three cheers for Dewey and every one
Who made Spains "noble boys" all run,
Who showed how thinghs should be properly done.
While fighting before Manila;

Three cheers for the hand who played "A Hot
Time in Town," while the enemy shot

At their water-wet forms, but they minded it not
While marching before Manila.

Never mind who tore down the enemy's rag;
Never mind who raised up our glorious Flag;
It went up quicker than tongues that wag
Under it bright in Manila.

Don't ask for official facts, you know,
So they who "retired in order" can go
Home to Spain as, "our heroes," and blow,
And brace up better than at Manila.

Three cheers for our Flag; for the Red, White and B'ue
For the greatest Nation God ever knew
Remember that, boys, and you'll ever be true,
In any old place in Manila.

Edward S. Paterson
1st North Dakota U. S. V.

WE'RE, NATURAL BORN SOLDIERS,

Oh! the order came down for the Battery to march,
The boys tore up the shirts, that were laundered with starch.
Put on the blue ones given to us,
And if it did not fit, why, we raised an awful fuss.
Put on our knapsack, haversacks too,
Canteens, revolvers and uniforms new.
Marched up Broadway keeping step well,
Did not mind the heat, though it was hot as   (Zum)

Chorus—We are natural born soldiers.
We are natural born soldiers.
We are natural born soldiers.
And that ain't   no   lie

We reached Camp Astor. a twenty mile walk
That famous march, is the talk of New York.
Pitched our camps with spirits gay

In the middle of a field of new mown hay,
I laid down lazy as 'a' Turk
We mounted the guard, then we stopped all work
Out came the buglers blew retreat
Come to find out, there was nothing to eat.   (Zum)

The first night out Oh? for home we did yearn,
Every man in the camp had blisters to burn,
We washed our feet, they were heavy as lead
Next morning all the fish in the brook were dead.
The Captain said, ration orders I received
For the next three days you can live on the breeze
But we found an old carpet, Oh! it was a funny crack
To see each one chew an old hard-tack.   (Zum)

On a Monday morn Oh: we broke camp
Started for Van Nest on a three mile tramp
The captain said as out the gate you pass
As we have no mules, each man must be an ass
To act like mules, we tried our best
We did it so well we never got a rest
In Van Nest on a gin-mill a sign said Malt,
Some one in the crowd cried "for goodnes sake halt,"   (Zum)

It was two fifteen when we reached Van Nest
We were told we would have ten minutes to rest,
Telegrams flew to New Jer-sey,
Saying meet me at the depot I ll be there at three,
They waited there you bet and we waited too,
Waited so long we were all getting blue,
When the band played The Star Spang'ed Banner in tune
Then we would have waited till the middle of june,   (Zum)

Oh ! we sailed down the river in the middle of the stream
You never heard in all your life, such a serenade of steam,
A hundred-whistles tooting a thousand lusty blows
The man who had no whistle, had to stop and blow his nose
We reached old Jer-sey City the train was waiting there
We hugged and kissed our sweethearts, there was smacking every where
Then three lusty cheeers w re given as the train it moved along
And we all joined in the chorus of our good old Battle song.   (Zum

At every little station in the Western towns so new
There a waited a reporter for a'stounding interview
"What is your name, and the date of your birth,?
Can you give me your excuse, for your presence on the earth ?
Are your parents wealthy, and how do you feel ?'
Are you a college graduate, an1 did you bring your wheel ?
When did you enlist and Oh ! wont you tell me why, ?
That was the time we'd turn' em down, with this reply.   (Zum)

Do you eat loose tomatoes with a knife or a fork,
You could stand there and starve while you listen to him talk
Strange it would be if he'd ever let you pass
With out some explanation about an ammunition case
A reporter came up to me, a country dude so cutes
Wanted to know if the Battery boys could shoot
I froze him with a look, as I jumped on the cars
Said I to him my friend, We're a band of shooting stars.

When the war is over it will be a mystery
If the doings of the Battery don't go down in history
How every single one of us gave up our homes so gay
And started for the battle field ten thousand miles a way,
When we are dead and gone our children will ta'k
Of the famous Astor Battery that started from New-York
A monument they'll build to us telling every deed
And those who stop to look at it will have a chance to read.   (Zum)

Chas. C. Web.ter
Astor Battery U. S. A.

THE HALLOWED GROUND.

(Inscribed to the American soldiers who are buried on the Island
of Luzon.)

In a far-off, tropic island, girt round by the Eastern seas,
Where fronded palm and mango are swept by the scented breeze,

Our boys, in their blankets coffined, sleep well in their silent graves.
Where the long, curved bey, till the Judgment Day, shall sound with
        its mournful waves.
Oh, sad were our hearts that morning when they brought them
        off from the field.
The servers who—God willed it—the utmost tithe must yield;
And we mourned for the men, our comrades, who foreign graves had
        found
And who had made of a savage shore God's well-beloved ground.

Oh, they were young and hopeful, and mothers or wives were theirs;
Oh, they were tenderly followed by yearnings and dreams and prayers.
Oh, but they thrilled in their glory when midst cheers they marched away
To the field of the dead and a narrow bed by the shores of the mur
        mnring bay.
Oh, they had hoped to triumph o'er sickness and death and fear
They meant to serve that they might deserve, returning, the lusty cheer
They dreamed of many a fireside scene when the strife should long
        be o'er.
But alas! they lie 'neath the tropic sky, asleep —God's spoil of war.

I dream of a far-off rustic town where a hill climbs up to the sky;
Of a dusty road where an eager boy from school comes tramping by,
I see on a grass-grown, silent street a cottage with rustic gate,
Where a mother stands with her work in her hands, her boy's return
        to 'wait.
And alas, alas! I see again the mother with eyes grown dim—
The "boys" are coming home from the war, and her boy—ah, what of
        him?
And the evening falls and the cricket calls through the shadows still and
        gray;
But the boy that is gone sleeps, on and on, by the far, surf-beaten bay,

Then God, who, hid in Thine unseen hands life's mysteries still
        doth keep;
Who giveth to one a vigil long-to another a longer sleep,
Oh, give to the mother, or give to the wife a song in the stilly night,
With soothing and rest to the empty breast, till dawn with its labor and
        light

And these graves? Oh, grander than shaft of steel they shall stand as a
    monument strong,
To say that the men of our native land shall never submit to wrong.
Columbia's sons shall ever avenge the men whom murderers slay,
And the world may read, and the lesson heed, in the graves by the
    blood stained bay,

Lou Bill Dodge
18th Infantry U. S. A.

A SOLDIER'S FAREWELL.

Air "Sweet Marie."

I am lying in my tent, Sweet Marie,
And my soul with rage is pent, up in G.
    For I know almighty well you have
      caught another fel.,
And your thoughts no longer dwell, love, with me.

When we kissed a last goodbye, tearfully,
You but worked a girlish guy off on me,
    O, you sweet, bewitching jade, what a
      clever game you played.
For your tears were ready made Sweet Marie.

Sweet Marie, list to me list to me, Sweet Marie.
While I whisper to the winds, you're n. g.
    You were icy I, you were true I was all
      the world to you,
When my cash for you I blew, Sweet Marie.

When I donned the soldier blue, Sweet Marie.
Like a picnic woodtick you stuck to me.
    And the smile you used to wear was as
      full of gleaming glare
As a sunbeam on a tear, Sweet Marie.

How your cunning head you'd lay, lovingly,
On my boson while you'd say things to me;
    These you'd rest in loving pose; right be..

neath my very nose.
Swiping buttons from my clothes, Sweet Marie.

To the Philippines I go Sweet Marie.
Where the tropic sun will glow over me,
    And I'll wander through the dells with
        the brown Manila belles,
Who are dressed in beads and shells, scantily.

There your face I'll soon forget, Sweet Marie,
I'll be frisky, you can bet as a flea.
    I'll be giddy I'll be gay, I will sing the
        hours away,
Ta-ra-ra boom de ay! Hully gee!

Geo. W. Moulton
Ist South Dakota U. S. V.

SLEEPING IN THE PHILIPPINES

One day I saw a gallant troop ship sailing
Wives and sweethearts waved a good bye from the shore
But alas this parting bore a tinge of sorrow
For amidst them there's a lad we'll see no more
And among the crowd a gray haired mother totters
For against her will her boy had gone to fight
Neath his uniform of blue beats his heart to country true
He's fighting in the Philippines to night.

Chorus—In far a way Manila where the fair palmetto grows
Where the Sun forever casts his golden light
In this land of sunshine gay in his mouldering grave of clay
He's sleeping in the Philippines to night.

But the months rolled by and till there came no message
That would bring her tidings of her darling boy
And the weary days past in sad succession
Yet no answer came to fill her heart with joy
But she cherishes the hope that still she'll see him
From her aged breast hope ne'er will take its flight

As the weary days crept past, she's still waiting but alas
He's sleeping in the Philippines to night

In far away Manila where the fair palmetto grows
Where the sun forever casts its golden light
In this land of sunshine gay'in his mould'ring grave of clay
He's sleeping in the Philippines to night

John M. Miller
1 st. California U. S. V.

NEBRASKA BOYS IN THE TRENCHES

A rifle shot sharp in the rank bamboo
   Gave a sudden and ominous warning,
And the bullet sang out as away it flew,
   "There'll be merry work ere the morning"

"Keep quiet, boys, now, for the pickets are out;
   They'll be in as soon as ther's danger;
Ther's not much cause in a shot or a shout
   To worry a toughened old ranger.

"We've had many a scrap on the old bald range
   When we've met with the Sioux and Comanches;
We'll show to the Spanish, just for a change,
   How we drove the reds off from our ranches.

"Yes, just for a change for all will agree
   We've lain long enough in the ditches
And slumped in the bog-mire over the knee
   Till we've ruined our government breeches.

We're in for it now for here come the boys,
   But don't be alarmed by a trifle;
It's not just the time for yelling or noise,
   Take a look at the lock of your rifle.

'Twas a terrible light in the wood at night,
   When the battle-fire blazed round Manila,

And the roar and the crash of the desperate fight
    Roused a terror from village to villa.

Now, there's silence supreme in the rank bamboo,
    Not a whisper or sound in the thicket,
Save the katydid singing the whole night through
    Or the chirp of a rollicking cricket,

But the Spaniards no more, in the Isle of Luzon
    May boast of their prowess or glory
For their fame and their prowess and glory are gone
    Save in flickering legend and story.

                Ira Kellogg
                1st Nebraska U. S. V.

A HOT TIME FOR MINNESOTA

Come along get you ready, for we are going to the war
But it's nothing new to Minnesota, for she's been there before
We are going to lick the Spaniards, who are anxious for a fight
But for some unknown reason they keep quite out of sight.

Chorus—Please oh Please Mr. Spaniard do not run
For now that we are started we are bound to have some fun
And when we reach the Philippines, we'll put you on the bum
There'll be a hot time in Manila that night

We left old Minnesota on the 16th day of May
The boys were feeling frisky and eager for the fray
We arrived in San Francisco, that city on the bay
It was there they did surround us and we heard the people say

Chorus—Come Boys, Come, Come drink our lager Beer
'Tis free for you if you have to stay a year
For Minnesota Boys we'll always have a cheer
There was a hot time in Frisco that night

We left San Francisco on the good old Ship "Para"
The sea was very heavy and the wind was rather raw

The boys got very sea sick and their grub they could not chaw
So the boys went down below, to their little beds of straw

    Chorus—Say Boys Say they kept us on our feet
We drilled on deck the same as on the street
"Redhorse" and "Bean Soup" is what we had to eat,
There was a poor time on board ship that trip. .

We arrived in Honolulu, that place you all know well
They gave us a grand reception and a dinner that was swell
And when they saw "Old Glory" the people all did yell
Three cheers for Minnesota Boys they'll give the Spaniards h —l

    Chorus – When the Honolulu Band began to play
Then we heard the Gopher Boys say,
Here, oh here, is where we'd like to stay,
There was a blow-out in Lulu that night.

We arrived at Luzon Island, and we anchored in the bay
The Concord steamed around us, and we heard the Captain say,
Santiago has fallen, and the Spanish fleet's no more,
But you'll surely have a hot time, when you land on shore

    Chorus—Oh how the boys that night did cheer and yell
When they saw the ships that Dewey fought so well
And we felt so proud of that we can not tell.
There was a hot time for Minnesota that night,

We all got in the small boats and they landed us on shore
We marched along together, till our feet were very sore,
At Camp Dewey we pitched our dogtents, in mud and rains,
And in spite of all our hardships, we got there just the same.

    Chorus—Boys, oh Boys, how the rain did pour,
But we did not care, you should have heard us snore,
We a woke next morning looking for Spanish Gore,
There was a wet time, in Camp Dewey, that night,

On the 13th day of August. Oh that was a glorious day
When they marched the 13th Minnesota in thie thickest of the fray

But "old Dewey's" Guns were booming and the Yankee bullet flew
And soon old Mr. Spaniard skipped the tra—la—lu.

Chouus.—Say—Boys Say, that was a glorious fight,
They had no chance, because we were right,
And their old yellow flag, was soon put out of sight,
And "Old Glory" soon floated on high."

Now we're in Manila, we will do the best we can
And not get discouraged in this God forsaken land,
Bnt we'll hope that McKinley will soon call us home,
To Dear old Minnesota, and our dear loved ones.

Chouus.—Cheer, boys Cheer, we gave the Spaniards h—l
And when we get home the story we will tell,
How Minnesota Boys, did their duty true and well,
There'll be a hot time in Minnesota some night,

Burt D. Carrier
13th Minnesota U. S. V.

THE FIRST DAY OUT

Midst heaving ship and rising swell,
I write again to you friend Dell,
And strive with all my might to tell
Of the hard times that I have passed
On board, since I, have seen you last.

We scarcely passed the harbor bar,
And yet could see the land afar,
When holding on to rail and spar,
Each seasick soldier, upward cast;
The remnants of his last repast

The officers w th golden straps,
The rifle men with kits and traps,
Gaze not upon the flag that flaps
So gaily in the evening breeze,
But faintly d--n their new disease,

The sailors that compose the crew,
H w! at the jolly boys in blue,
And ask us if we still are true
To every patriotic toast,
We drank upon that distant coast.

Now, let me end this foolish theme,
Its o'er but lingers as a dream;
Far outward, to our goal we steam
Still holding in our hearts enshrined
Dear faces we have left behind.

Wm. H. Doyle
1st Montana U. S. V.

THE OREGON VOLUNTEER
AIR, NELLY GREY.

We are volunteers for freedom,
We've remembered well the Maine,
We came west o'er the rolling of the sea;
We have heard the battle's thunder
And we've seen the fall of Spain
Now we long for our home-land of the free.

Chorus—Oh, Oregon our home,
Sweet Oregon so fair,
For thy beauty we will e'er remember thee
We'll recross the rolling billows
To our Oregon so dear
And our loved ones in that home-land of the free.

We have seen our flag unfurling
From the shore to distant shore
We have seen our glorious colors borne afar
We have seen the famous Dewey
And his proud ship Baltimore
And his sqadron that fought the Spanish war.

Now we're waiting only waiting

For the order to return
To our homes in that land beyond the sea
For the flame of love for Oregon
Shall e'er be seen to beam,
Oregon, in that home.land of the free

McNail Howell
2nd Oregon U. S. V.

A SOLDIER'S RECOLLECTIONS

The bugles blast has called retreat
  The sun is sinking low,
The sentinel upon his beat
  Is pacing to and fro,
The River Pasig gently flows
  Beneath the tropic trees,
And Columbia oe'r the barrack throws
  Her banner to the breeze.

Quartered upon the river bark
  We now can take our ease,
While sweet the evening zephyrs come
  A whispering through the leaves.
The sun's last rays are falling now
  Upon the flowers and rills,
And far away to eastward
  They linger on the hills.

Back amid the under-brush
  The native planter dwells,
And there amid the evenings hush
  He wanders through the dells:
Those dells where but a few days past
  The angry cannon roared,
And where the haughty Spaniard cast
  To earth his bloody sword.

In evening's hour of quietude
  Fond thoughts are on the wind,
Of a nation and her gratitude

— 32 —

And loved ones left behind
For in our slumbers we can see
    The loved ones left at home,
And look far back across the sea
    Where billows dash and foam.

Beneath the dark banana tree's
    The guards their vigils keep,
While upon the barrack floor
    The soldiers go to sleep;
Oh sweetest thoughts and sweetest dreams,
    Of home and native land;
It's once again we seem to press
    Columbia's golden strand

                    Chas. Smith.
                    1st South Dakota U. S. V.

THE ARMY

I went into a recruiting place
The officer in charge, locked me square in the face,
He said "young man do you want to enlist?
If so please take off your pants coat and vest"
A quack army Doctor examined my frame,
He pounded my chest until I was lame,
Now if I get a chance I will cave in his brain
And he won't prescribe pills any more.
Chorus—In the Army—the Army
They call you a rockey and feed you on soupey
        In the Army the Army

I guess I will enlist again—NIT   (spoken)

We have pork and beans three times a day
My friends I tell you I'd rather eat hay,
We drill for four hours every day
It's to much drilling for such small pay
You leave your tent open and when you get back
Your minus a blanket and haversack
You can call me a lobster when I get back
If I go in the army again......

Chorus.—In the Army the Army
If you miss reveille from oversleep,
They will give you two days as kitchen police
    In the Army the Army

    I've had enough of it in mine.
On the first of May in Manila Bay
Dewey and Montejo played philopena they say
It was yes or no for a present grand
Dewey he lost, paid his debt like a man
The present he gave Montejo was shot and shell
He blew the Don's fleet straight to *hell*
If the Germans get gay he will whip them as well
Or any other nation on earth
Chorus
    Manila Manila

Where the scrappy Fourteenth is always on hand
They will fight until they lose their last man
In Manila,   Manila
The worst place that God ever made
Now that we're here we must obey
To what "Shoulders Straps" and Non-Com's say
But such is life so what can you do
They know that they have the bulge on you
Just wait till we're free from the goverment yoke
We can tell them to go where there's plenty of smoke
It's then we'll get even and that's no joke
Their stripes will not bother us then.

Chorus In America America
Where every body has a fair show
You dont need a pass to go to and fro
In America America
The land of the Free, Brave and True.

                Walter Commerce.
                14th Infantry U. S. A.

5

CALIFORNIA VOLUNTEERS

Whose parapetted walls are those
    Which overhang Manila bay!
Whose fortressed towers that sentinel
    Entombments since Magellan's day

Tall sentries pace the ramparts now
    With soldierly and buoyant mien;
The Stars and Stripes forevermore
    Shall float the church and state between.

For yesterday proud Spain was there
    In war's Iberian panoply
Where now the boys of UNCLE SAM
    Stand forth for peace and liberty.

Monarchial splendor thus subdued
    To godly Freedom's mighty host!
America, so fair, so true,
    Thy children sacrifice the most.

Whene'er those youngest sons of Mars
    Returning sail from far Luzon
Their pathway shall be lit by love—
    Fond mother's love, as always shone.

And when, among the garlanded
    We welcome them with joyous cheers,
Our own dear boys shall be the first—
    Fair California Volunteers.

              J J. Galvin
              1st Wyoming U. S. V.

THE GIRL WITH DARK RED HAIR

The Pennsylvanie slowly heaves
It's anchor from the brine.
This is the day Montana leaves,
To help a cause divine,
And as we gently plow along
Where cheering rends the air,
We see among the eager throng
A Girl with dark red hair

She is bright as a morning star,
Fair in the light of day,
Cheering us on our way to war:
Out far out and away.
Standing there on a tow boat's bow
A vision sweet and rare,
The spray from off the plung ing prow
Touching the dark-red hair.

As on the transport quickly flyes
And ill the wind behaves.
Regardless of our warning cries;
The dashing sea she braves,
Drenched with the ever rising spray;
That sparkles in the air,
The center of that bright display
The Girl with dark red hair

Out by the world famed Golden Gate
Where bay and ocean meet,
We glide along to find our fate,
If it be slow or fleet,
In battles strife or on the wave.
Within our hearts we'll wear,
An image sweet and fair and brave;
A Girl with dark red hair,

Wm   H. Doyle
1st. Montana U. S. V.

ON THE DECKS OF THE PEKING

Round our floating palace dewlling wash the wild waves.
Above us exist air and ozone free,
But that is all we get upon the Peking
And we've yet a month to spend upon the sea.
When on the deck we sit and think of Frisco
Of the happy homes we all have left behind
Within our breats arise the sorest feelings
For we're treated worse than felons lcw confined

Chorus.—O it may be well to shout of Volunteering
And go marching down the street to drum and fife
But this death by slow starvation,s quite annoying
And we'd enlist again—not on your life!

On the spar deck we assembled every morning.
After spending all the night in Tuikish bath;
To each man they give a brscuit and some coffee
That would make a starving dog rise up in wrath.
The Majors and the Captains live on dainties
Served by flui k es in the dining hall below
While we poor suckers live on hog and glory
Those who grabbed their guns have got to swallow crow.

We thought when we our good right hand uplifted
And swore to take the treacherous Dons to tak
That to each man at least there would be given
Enough to eat—that's all we want and ask
We would not kick if grub could not be gotten
But its everywhere aronnd us boxed uptight
And it makes us sore to live on what we're given
With so much to eat aboard and within sight.

E. B. Lenhart
1st California U. S. V.